KERRY C

NOT OVERKEPT POEMS
POEMS

VOLUME ONE

This is a work of the imagination. In other words, I made it up
and no one should get bent out of shape over content.

ISBN-13: 978-0-9769765-7-8

Printed in the United States of America

First Printing: November 2021

25 24 23 22 21   5 4 3 2 1

Published by:
five friends books™

fivefriendsbooks.com

CONTENTS

CONTENTS

RULES OF NOT OVERLY POETIC POEMS

Poems can be cloudy
Poems can be sunny

Poems can be gritty
Poems can be witty

Poems can be straight
Poems can be wending

Poems can be lyrical
Poems can be farcical

Poems can be understated
Poems can be overrated

Poems can rhyme
Or not

But just for the record
Poems are not a place
To take your trash
For weekly
Curbside collection

We clear
William Shakespeare?

TO-DON'T

We go through life
making lists
and we go through lists
making checkmarks.
Perhaps it's time
for a list flip-flop.

Today's to-don't list:
Overthink it
Look at your phone so much
Confuse possessions with success
Underestimate the nap
Hold grudges
Deflect compliments
Blow through yellow lights
Keep score
Go down a political rabbit hole
Round down the tip
Stuff your dreams in a shoebox
Decline bacon

BESIDE MOM

Crosswalk
Yellow light
Fast slapping bare feet
He jiggled across
August's scorched street

Damp faded beach towel
Sunburned shoulders
Maybe he's all of twelve
Quite overweight
Like that needed to be said
And said and said
Wave after wave
Of bullying at the public pool

Athletic Nick
And his all-star entourage
Prematurely muscle-chested
Silver Catholic crosses around their necks
They finally pushed him
Up and over and out

He and Mom
Hurried homeward now
Waddled really
Below the impatient yellow traffic light
That switched to red

A block from the public pool
Hotter than hell
No shade to be found for
"Beached whale blubber boy!"
Except the one
Shade
More powerful than their cannon words

Beside Mom
That shade
At twelve
Gets you to thirteen
A lot can happen from there

OPEN WIDE

Won't wear no mask
in the land of the free
socialist nanny bullshit
don't lecture me.

I'm one hundred percent
American made
steel on the inside
not afraid.

I'll say what I want
open my mouth
the virus jumped in
it's not coming out.

Ain't old and weak
mostly healthy
not changing my life
let's party.

The ambulance doors
swing open wide
narrow-minded man
placed inside.

Won't wear no mask
in the land of the free
don't need one now
the virus got me.

OVERHEARD

Just to set the stage
our house is small.

From my office
one floor above our living room
separated only by a single
open
flight of stairs
I overheard my wife
ask my college freshman son—
quite enthusiastically
about the upcoming semester:

"Have you had sex before?"

He: "No."
She: "I think you'll like it."
He: "Yeah. I'm excited." PAUSE. "I hear it's hard."
She: "I think you'll be good at it."

As sweat began to amass
I realized the word she had said was:

"Stats."

RAISING A STINK

something remains stuck
inside 1600 Pennsylvania Avenue
where number one
has been declared number two

our resolve remains firm
as we grip the handle
plunge away
light a candle

TOUGH ROUND

Golf is like
a dinner party
where you put on a collared shirt
arrive on time
are greeted by friends
engage in lively conversation
breathe in stunning surroundings
and when you're called to dinner
you come to the table
begin to sit down
and the chair gets
yanked out from beneath you.

Nice, golf.
Real nice.

LADDERS

His piercings and tats and ladders go high
Been nine months since the bottle went dry

Stenciled sign, sun-blasted, fading
A phone number and the words Devin's Painting

A house is restored one stroke at a time
People too when they make up their mind

Scraping, sanding, determination
A fresh coat replaces humiliation

Devin sat in the shade, had a smoke
Neighbors strolled by but never spoke

He mulled over a Bible verse
Be reborn or hail a hearse

Pastor Wes promises a different clean
Where stains and prison records go unseen

How high will a ladder take him?
Can a pail of paint hold redemption?

A rung at a time, upward Devin
I'm thinking he gets to heaven

SOLSTICE

Streetlights just flickered on
spring's luminous days long past
sky dim, worn flat
dark convening fast.

Window dances in golden light
where mother and baby sway
lampshade stands like a hoopskirt
day fades away.

High-rise apartment, happy hour
elder residents arrive on the dot
couples whose marriages have survived
battles armies could not.

Bow-tied ringleader hoists a glass
to bygone days, departed friends
aged whiskey sparks temporary youth
as the short days of December end.

HIKING

For a man
of a certain age
"hiking"
involves not lacing boots
nor watering a canteen
and does not enlist one's
calves or quads
into service.

No sir.
This hiking
refers to the steady upward
climb
of a man's
trousers.

The beltline
hiking
ascending
heaven bound
beyond hips
pulling
to the summit
atop
the belly
to the sternum!

Oh, great pants
you hike.

HIKING

Soon I will be kissed
by the waistband
as you climb higher
higher yet
and suffocate
me—
death
by dungarees.

MAGICAL WINTER MORNING

There will be no race to the coffeepot
this morning
the family has slept in.

I've returned from my early trek
through white-gowned pines
my dog in front, breaking trail.

Inside our cozy cabin
a Frasier fir erect in the great room
is festooned with ornaments
like sparkling breadcrumbs marking
our sons' twenty-one and eighteen Christmases
here.

In this winter oasis
we slide wooden pieces across game boards
feast on cookies and books
pull large fish through dark holes in the ice
there is no television.

While my dog nips ice from her pads
I remove my coat
an occasional catching wheeze in my chest
where once there was
only bravado.

Too soon this string will break
and my heart with it
as our Christmas week will
relocate somewhere busy and green.

But I will be here
if for a moment
walking beneath a white flurry
descending earthward like a scattered poem
torn into scraps
by the creator
for me to piece together
before they melt.

ANNIVERSARY

Numbness
wanders his soul
loss
swift and impossible
haunts the farmer's frozen ground.

Rage
that land could not bury
whorling
trees moaning
took the bark off the man.

Empty
he's smoking again now
silence
where they played pom-pom-pullaway.

Wrecked
the farmer does what he does
turns his back to the wind
puts up his hood
and takes the bullwhip.

CONTRARY

She's a big woman
He's a small man
She's a seat-of-the-pants gal
He prefers a plan

She'll sit and talk
He likes his walks
She seeks activities
He avoids festivities

She hates a mess
He couldn't care less
How they stay together
Is anyone's guess

What one lacks
The other makes up
So together
They have enough

She believes in extraterrestrials
He says that's hysterical
She plays the lottery
He prays for miracles

She's quick to hold hands
He'd rather just stand
She likes country ballads
He listens to Chopin

CONTRARY

They had detractors
These opposite attractors
But love has the last say
Happy fiftieth anniversary

NEWS

COVID. COVID. COVID. COVID. COVID. COVID.
COVID. COVID. COVID. COVID. COVID. COVID.
COVID. COVID. COVID. COVID. COVID. COVID.
COVID. COVID. COVID. COVID. COVID. COVID.
COVID. COVID. COVID. COVID. COVID. COVID.
COVID. COVID. COVID. COVID. COVID. COVID.
COVID. COVID. COVID. COVID. COVID. COVID.
COVID. COVID. COVID. COVID. COVID. COVID.
Quarantine sheep gets epic haircut loses 78 pounds.
COVID. COVID. COVID. COVID. COVID. COVID.
COVID. COVID. COVID. COVID. COVID. COVID.
COVID. COVID. COVID. COVID. COVID. COVID.
COVID. COVID. COVID. COVID. COVID. COVID.
COVID. COVID. COVID. COVID. COVID. COVID.
COVID. COVID. COVID. COVID. COVID. COVID.
COVID. COVID. COVID. COVID. COVID. COVID.
COVID. COVID. COVID. COVID. COVID. COVID.

VALENTINE'S DAY

Why do two lives intersect
and fuse in love?
What power arranges this?

Many of us remember
the first time
I saw her
I saw him
I saw they—
(pick a pronoun)

Indeed the creator
must relish
this first moment of intersection.
Does the maker say
to a nearby apprentice:
"Hey, watch what I'm going to do here"?

REMEMBERING FEBRUARY 22, 2017: OLATHE, KANSAS

Wrinkled and white
he had a pillowcase
face
Whiskered in lies
two shit stains
for eyes

A hateful man
gun in hand
He heard the President
inciting anguish
they'll steal your jobs
but won't speak our language

It's them or you
you know what to do

The man mumbled things
hard to tell
until he unbridled
a rebel yell

Get out of my country!
alien bastard
you're half nigger
half retard

REMEMBERING FEBRUARY 22, 2017: OLATHE, KANSAS

The gun exploded
repeated times
life unloaded
in a hate crime

Tackled to the floor
the gunman roared
where he lay in a flood
of three men's blood

Not alien green
not Muslim black
but red as his own
red as the local resident's
red as the President's

DOG BOOKS

I bought a few books
not for me
my dog was bored
sleep sleep sleep
I wanted her to have
something constructive to do.

One book was on England.
One was about volleyball.
The last was *The Rules
of Etiquette.*

I left her to them
and dashed off to work.

Total backfire.
Now my dog wants to be
an English Setter
who won't point.

OVERTURES

Boots slosh
February melts
Minnesota hasn't known
forty-six degrees
in forever

Coats
unzipping
tires
hydroplaning
downspouts
alive with snowmelt
like tubas
filled with spit

Wonderful long
lost sounds

Our sun
closing in

Spring
working up the nerve
to ask
to come home again

EARLY ONSET

closet door open
pantry door open
silverware drawer open
cupboard door open

microwave door open
freezer door open
trash bin door open
dryer door open

porch door open
garage door open
car door open
front door open

when he shuffles off
to the sweet hereafter
bet on it
behind him
the pearly gates
will be left open

DYE HOMONYMS, DYE!

Homonyms
who kneads 'em?

It's hard to right
write

With these
sound a likes

Hay even my editor
misses one or too

What am eye
two dew?

Dadgum
homonyms

I'm threw
with ewe!

EMANCIPATION

I was thinking about a bike tire
how the owner rides above it
moving forward in a straight line
and the tire goes around
and around and around.

And how the owner is alive
in the exuberance
of racing ahead in a straight line
and the tire goes around
and around and around.

Owner
bike tire
moving through the same space and time
completely differently.

For the tire to experience
the rowdy joy of advancing ahead
in a straight line
someone has to slam on the BRAKES!

The next time you see a protest
think about the bike tire.

STUCK

seeing the Ever Given
stuck in the Suez
what metaphor
should I reach for?

it's like a fishbone
in the throat of commerce
or a sea of Metamucil
proving futile

it's like a cursor blinking
on a blank page
or a word unsung
on the tip of the tongue

it's like being down on your luck
hopelessly stuck
rescued by a full moon's lift
and tugboats of friendship.

BLOW YOUR LID

Tupperware bumfuzzle
I shake my fist at you
at containers clear
at containers blue.

Bottoms don't fit the top
tops don't fit the bottom
by the time I find a match
my leftovers are rotten.

They tumble from the cabinet
a mishmash of aggravation
are they multiplying in there
wild plastic fornication?

To keep food fresh
is the Tupperware pledge
I suspect a darker conspiracy:
push humanity over the edge.

OCEAN COLORS

fingers pinched in blue beach chairs
wedding rings and silver hair

from churning surf leaps pewter fish
snowy egret gets her wish

spiral shells painted in saltwater
red floppy hats on mom and daughter

sapphire waves curl for land
watched by sunburned umbrella man

with sandy toes I take this look
at nature's gulf-side coloring book

THE STREET

There's an older man
across the street
nice enough guy, helpful
walks over as the day darkens
tells me I left my headlights on or
the drain spout is detached and
rain's coming of the variety
that floods basements.

These kinds of things are easy to miss
when you're chasing kids and careers and
racing out the door for practice
with microwaved hotdogs
wrapped in paper towels.

I appreciate the older man and how
he has time to notice such things…

No wait, crap.
I'm the older man now.
How did I cross *that* street?

FULL

Minnesota air full of smoke
European roadways full of river
Pacific Northwest full of wildfire
Greenland coastline full of melt
Farmers' fields full of wither
World's oceans full of hurricanes
Schoolkids' backpacks full of inhalers
Amazon rainforest full of carbon
Senators' offices full of lobbyists
Next generation full of dread
Climate change deniers full of shit

QUIET CABIN WALK

the wind is out of the north today
it doesn't come alone
bringing octaves of birdsong
woodpecker's jackhammer
angry ratchet of a red squirrel

my shadow scrapes the blacktopped road
until panting dog and I
turn onto an old logging trail
forest duff dampens our steps
dog, birdy, pointing, I expect a grouse
instead, I'm nearly shot out of my boots by
a flushing turkey

the gobbling brute
a helicopter liftoff in contrast to the stillness
lumbering wings slapping tree limbs of the
understory
until he ascends through the canopy

in the regained silence
one feather pirouetting down
from the wild blue above
proving quite spectacularly
if a feather falls in a forest
and someone is around to hear it
it makes a sound

REENTRY

Life went virtual
and lost its luster
months dragged on
like a filibuster

Muted trumpets
we wore our masks
tuned in Fauci
did as asked

We got our shots
right arm or left
that's as political
as it should get

The countdown is on
to reenter society
here's the trick
to calm anxiety

Ignore the missing heat shields
forget the infrared roof
make your smile easy-going
and your sweatpants fireproof

SHADDUP

Tall oak
branches veining
into a blanched sky
black crow

Green hillock
trotting up and down
like a sine wave
brown dog

From above
the crow
caw caw caw caw caw
incessant

From below
the dog
bark bark bark bark bark
obnoxious

Crow holds its perch
Dog stands its ground

CAW! BARK! CAW! BARK! CAW! BARK!

Politics

BACKING

Words are said
under extreme duress
in times of war, childbirth
and I must confess

When backing up a camper
there'll be some cursing
as things go sideways
while reversing

A crowd gathers
kids point popsicles at me
as I nearly
flatten a tree

"Right!" "Left!" "Stop!"
"Okay, okay!"
the eagle has landed
long day

Finally in place
unfolding camp chairs
inaugural fire snaps
in the fresh air

That night you'll drift off
to the sweetest dream
finest camper backer-upper
this park's ever seen

INTROVERT

You
reluctant moon
you
hider of light.

There you are again
behind clouds
trying to diminish
your brilliance.

You cannot conceal it
disappear behind it
deflect or deny it.

A brushstroke of fog
levitates like a silver goddess
above the field's hollow
only because you shine down.

Can you not see
this magnificence
cannot compare to
reluctant
you?

JULIA

under the shadow of a birch
beside the peeling church
gravestone high on a hill
she leaned on the Coupe de Ville

Grandpop left her the keys
said she should leave
because dreams drown
in this backwater town

sunglasses white rims
Julia's face thin
trunk packed with stuff
saw her future from this bluff

punch a clock
marry a jock
swap recipes
pop babies
it's a slow dance
with ignorance

opening a Coke
on the road to hope
pedal to the metal
alleluia, Julia

HUMAN DISHWASHER

What if you could hold Earth in your hands
like you can a bowl
passed down by your grandmother?

To wash it, you wouldn't banish it
to some soulless stainless steel appliance
instead
you and suds and sponge and care
would soap and rinse Mother Earth by hand
for those who come next.

It's the right thing to do.

This is how I mini-lectured my second son
who hacked on me for the zillionth time
for my no-dishwasher-at-the-cabin policy.

He then showed me a Google article called
Automatic Dishwasher More Water-Efficient And
Earth-Friendly Than Washing Dishes By Hand.

I then showed him a Google article called
Shut Up And Dry.

FORE! BECOMES FOUR

The mathematician and the golfer
are kindred
in their reverence for numbers
yet math and golf often disagree.

While both practitioners
can calculate and chew gum
the mathematician's numbers add up
whereas the golfer's are known to add down.

There are golf shots you want to forget
that somehow get forgotten
allowing 1+1+1+1+1 to equal 4
making your math subpar
but you just parred that hole
proving that bad math
often makes for good golf.

CONCRETE MAN

in front of the house
curves a new walkway
concrete man
poured today

little boy next door
fascinated, watches
laborer kneels
trowels gray swatches

an ache is awakened
by this nearby child
concrete man and his son
have not reconciled

words they spat
hardened between them
five years
unforgiven

by child and by walkway
the universe has spoken
lay down your grievance
repair what's broken

PREVIOUSLY

history has strong hands
shaping us
clumsily as often as
wisely

if we wince or smile
embody ignorance or guile
flamboyance or reticence
know that we are determined
by earlier episodes

this Netflix series
called life
began many seasons ago
for you and for me

be good with where you find yourself
we are the past in the present
we are previously

HOOKED

I close my eyes
and a river opens
in the upper reaches
of my mind

into cobalt and silver
I wade a world underwater
green weeds switching like mares' tails
black boulders tattooed by canoe paint

current pulls me
toward a distant applause of riffles
to a deep pool
smooth surface stirring

ghostly dry fly
hackle small as a freckle
lands gentle
dead drifts until

like a cap blown off a cola bottle
quiet erupts
a finned tornado
a striking rainbow

maybe now you see
why man and trout
are both hooked
on the Brule

JOB IN CHICAGO

There is thunder
in my heart today
departure
stuffed in boxes
all around

Child grows
unroots
packs up
the life I fathered
turns away

Lithely he moves
beckoned by a whisper
from the future
leaving me stuck
as a piano key

At the window I'm left
watching through branches
car rolls off
without a moment's
hesitation

SPUDDERINGS

Do you ever wake up feeling low
as a potato
lumpy, lackluster, indistinguishable
from the rest of the sack?
Hey now
Solanum tuberosum
out of dirt you rose
and from your starchy plinth
the gastronomical equivalent of
Michelangelo's David is sculpted.
In a world of boiled rice
you are a crispy chip
you are a twice-baked potato
you are the pommes frites!

Note:
If words fail to lift your spirits
substitute curly fries.

ENOUGH

How many square feet of house
or rungs on a career ladder
or followers on social media
or inches off a waistline
or commas in a bank account
are enough?

When the light
finally leaks out of us
the only *enough* that endures
is that we made enough time
for others
or we didn't.
The rest amounts to a frog fart
in the cosmos.

LEFT TO CHILDREN

Eye color
Winterizing an engine
Flaky apple pie crusts
Table manners
Lilac bushes

When we go
old boats, cut rope
released from our moors
what will have sunk in?

"Doesn't *that* remind you
of Mom? Of Dad?"

Fresh popped popcorn
Windex squeegee squeak
Smoldering charcoal
Cards shuffling
Gravel road

Be assured
we will endure
in memories
left deep
as treasure

START WITH YES

daydreams for breakfast
help a neighbor for lunch
indulge the usual victims
of our time crunch

say yes more than no
while your heart is whole
go out for waffles
buy tickets to the show

oh baby
assassinate maybe
because heartbreak
is at the gate

a collapsed swing set
a malfunctioning jet
a certain kind of hell
in a cancer cell

close your computer
rally some friends
don't count your blessings
spend them

AUGUST 24, 1996

It doesn't have to be perfect
this union of ours
to be radiant.

You and I
we are like candle
and match
fork and knife
coffee and mug
child and bubblegum
squeak and porch swing.

You didn't just come across
a gymnasium floor for me
you crossed six states
south to north.

Now twenty-five years
paired we transition
our next season
trees nudging crimson.

We move in tandem
you and I
like winter
and blankets.

NEED RAIN

Blistering bellowing arid wind
blows across tinderbox terrain
pastor became a fireworks peddler
sure hope we get that rain

Fake news holy hell
steeple cracks off the church
withering fields bear no wheat
religion in reverse

Baptism river bone dry
bellwether stampedes the flock
dust swirling in suspension
mayhem a ticking clock

Unholy water Kool-Aid thirst
democracy's steps are stormed
truth crushed, left for dead
disinformation now the norm

Parched soul country splits
the rapt a runaway train
pastor lights the attack fuse
sure hope we get that rain

LABOR DAY

Best friends
two thin-legged boys
astride bikes
grocery store parking lot
Cheetos bag
between them

One in a yellow helmet
wears glasses
one in a black helmet
multi-colored sandals
sun-smacked blacktop
catches crumbs

Pale blue sky
cottontail clouds
orange fingers happily cling
to the last days of a summer
gone almost as fast
as a bag of Cheetos

THANKFUL

They uncork wine
a bottle at a time
the pinot grigio syndicate
plot their next hit.

Julie walks funny
Kayla: not enough money
as for Claire
have you seen that hair?

And please not Donna
with her recent drama
won't have that sinner
at the ladies club dinner.

God no not Jules
they attend public school
and cross off Jennifer
she laughs like a woodchipper.

Words are their shiv
passive aggressive
voices pour sweet and delicate
from the pinot grigio syndicate.

The hostess takes a sip
and there at her hip
is the word THANKFUL
stitched on a pillow.

THANKFUL

Who could have known
in one word sewn
so abundant the irony
in a bit of embroidery?

NOT IN TODAY'S WORLD

Jack and Jill went up the hill
to fetch a pail of water...

Actually, it wasn't Jack and Jill
because Jack is with William now
which is basically why Jill backed over
Jack's $7000 carbon-fiber road bike
before driving to Fargo to help her pregnant sister.

And it's common knowledge there's no water up that hill
because Jack's grandpop and Jill's grandma have been
feuding over water rights
since the river got diverted by developers
to irrigate the new 36-hole private golf complex in town
ironically named Cascading River.

Plus, nobody in their right mind was going up that hill
ever since the deranged Boogaloo Bois tweeted about
holding Civil War exercises in the pasture just to the south
brandishing "full insurrection erections."

And seriously...returning to the nursery rhyme's premise
young Jack and Jill aren't going up any hill
unless Mom drives them in her Range Rover
or if their phones get four bars from there.

WIND

People who don't care for
wind
haven't watched you comb down
knee-high grass like
Sunday school hair
nor have they spread their arms to you
like a kite.

People who don't care for
wind
haven't watched you lift a dog's ears
nor heard you
snap laundry on the line.

Wind
I admire how you paint white manes
on galloping lake waves
and push ghosts on vacant swings.

Wind
I applaud
your tomfoolery
getting me to chase my hat
down the road.

LESS IS MORE

I want more E. coli in my potato salad
I want more toxins in my rain
I want more children working in my factories
I want more pesticides killing my pollinators
I want more second-hand smoke in my tavern
I want more impoverished citizens in my country
I want more malpractice in my hospitals
I want more assault rifles in my shopping malls
I want more unsupported veterans in my community
I want more microplastics in my ocean
I want more terrorists destabilizing my global economy
I want more seven-dollar-an-hour jobs in my economy
I want more infestation in my food processing plants
I want more dark money in my elections
I want more greenhouse gasses in my atmosphere
I want more crude oil on my beaches
I want more deterioration of my infrastructure
I want more coal-burning plants in my backyard
I want more loopholes for my rich CEO
I want more monopolies gouging prices beyond my means
I want more hungry kids in my schools
I want more subprime mortgage defaults in my economy
I want more PFCs in my drinking water
I want more pandemics in my world

I want less government in my life

RAIN SPARK

I puncture the air
with the tip of a pen
onto the page
words fall again

Stanzas sprinkle my mind
I read them aloud
listening for the rhythm
of rain from a cloud

Cupping hands around
the kindling to write
despite the dampness
something ignites

Every poem needs a spark
something beautiful or plain
today I find mine
kept inside by rain

GOODBYE

While her boys sleep
their mother weeps.

Bedside
family leans
as life machines
monitor and dispense
in hollow cadence.

A body
can be kept alive
but if you can't live
bighearted
and the soul has
departed
it's time
to whisper goodbye
knowing
children will rise
tears will dry
and within us all
her life
will reside.

THE FIRE NEEDS TENDING

You strike a match
made in heaven
flames intertwine
hearts leaven.

One minute
everything's roaring
before you know it
the duet is snoring.

Work, kids, collapse
you're getting older
easy to rationalize
the encroaching smolder.

Newlyweds, geezers
love's not unending
word to the wise
the fire needs tending.

READERS' COMMENTS

Readers value what other readers have to say about a book—as do I. While these *Not Overly Poetic Poems* are still fresh in your mind, please go to fivefriendsbooks.com and share your thoughts in the Readers' Comments section. Thanks.

Novels by Kerry Casey

The Wager
Runt
Slender Wish
Singer
Fall to Grace

Learn more at **fivefriendsbooks.com**

Made in the USA
Monee, IL
03 December 2021

82764805R00069